STEP-BY-STEP

50 Rainy Day Projects for Kids

STEP-BY-STEP

50 Rainy Day Projects for Kids

Petra Boase

Recipes by Sam Dobson
Photography by James Duncan

SMITHMARK

PUBLISHER'S NOTE

Crafts and hobbies are great fun to learn and can fill hours of rewarding leisure time, but some points should be remembered for safety and care of the environment.

• Always choose non-toxic materials wherever possible, for example paint, glue and varnishes. Where these are not suitable use materials in a well-ventilated area and always follow manufacturers' instructions.

• Needles, scissors and all sharp tools should be handled with care. Always use a cutting board or mat to avoid damage to surfaces (it is also safer to cut into a firm, hard surface).

• Protect surfaces from paint and glue splashes by laying down old newspapers.

SOME USEFUL TERMS

UK	US
card	*cardboard*
kitchen roll	*paper towel*
PVA glue	*white glue*
sticky-tape	*cellophane tape*

This edition published in 1994 by
SMITHMARK Publishers Inc.
16 East 32nd Street
New York
NY 10016

SMITHMARK books are available for bulk purchase for sales promotion and for premium use. For details write or call the Manager of Special Sales, SMITHMARK Publishers Inc. 16 East 32nd Street, New York, NY, 10016; (212) 532–6600.

ISBN 0 8317 8056 8

Produced by Anness Published Limited
1 Boundary Row
London SE1 8HP

Editorial Director: Joanna Lorenz
Series Editor: Lindsay Porter
Designer: Peter Laws
Photographer: James Duncan
Stylist: Madeleine Brehaut

Typeset by MC Typeset Ltd, Rochester, Kent
Printed and bound in Italy

CONTENTS

INTRODUCTION

It's raining again, and you've read all your books and played with all your toys so what can you do now? Rather than wait for the rain to stop and the sun to shine, why not make some of the exciting projects shown in this book?

Before getting to work on the projects, make sure you read the section on 'Getting Started'. This will tell you how to have fun without making too much mess and having an accident. In some of the projects such as baking Salt Dough or Potato Printing you will need the help of an adult.

One of the best parts of making the projects is collecting the materials from around the home. You will be amazed at what you can find. It's a good idea to keep a box for collecting toilet rolls, cereal boxes, egg cartons, newspaper and plastic bottles. In a short time, you will have collected all sorts of goodies which can be used in the projects.

If you find that you do not have all the materials required for a project, make use of those you already have. For example, if you only have a few colours of paint, try mixing them to create different colours. Red and yellow make orange, and blue and yellow make green.

So whether you are feeling hungry, playful or artistic, there is plenty here for you to do. Just use your imagination, have some fun and forget about the rainy day!

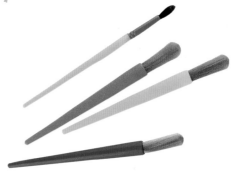

Getting Started

All the projects in this book can be made easily at
home, although some may need adult help. Before you
start, read the instructions below to make sure you
don't make too much of a mess, and don't have an
accident. Remember to ask permission before starting
a project and collecting all your materials – you don't
want to 'recycle' items which are actually new!

Right: *To prevent your clothes
from getting covered in paint
and glue, wear a smock or
apron, or ask an adult for
an old shirt. That way, you
can make as much mess as
you like!*

Left: *When you have decided
which projects you are going
to make, lay out all the
materials you will
need on your work
surface. You will
then find it
much easier to
get to work.*

Below: *Before you start work on any project, cover the surface you will be working on with newspaper or an old piece of material.*

Above: *If you can find a clear surface to work on, you'll find it much easier to make your projects. If you are using a desk or kitchen table, clear everything away before you begin so you have plenty of room.*

Left: *It is very important to keep all art materials away from your mouth. Not only will they taste very unpleasant, but they could also be dangerous.*

Materials and Equipment

These are just some of the materials used in this book.

Badge pins
These are glued onto the backs of badges. They can be bought from specialist shops.

Coloured pencils and crayons
These come in a huge range of colours and should be non-toxic.

Coloured sticky-tape
This is a strong tape which can be used for fastening heavy materials.

Crêpe and tissue paper
These come in lots of colours and can be used for making and decorating projects.

Cress seeds
These are scattered on moist cotton wool (balls) and left to grow into cress.

Face paints
These are used for decorating the face and body and can be removed easily with soap or cleansing cream.

Felt
This can be used in sewing projects. It is easy to cut and won't go ragged at the edges.

Felt-tip pens
These are always good to use on paper. The colours can't

be mixed like paint, so it's best to use them separately.

Flour
This is one of the ingredients used for making salt dough.

Glitter
This can be glued onto projects as decoration. If there is any left over it can be poured back in the tube.

Needle and thread
These are used to sew with. Needles are very sharp so you must be careful not to hurt yourself. Threads come in a large range of colours.

Paintbrushes
These are used for applying paint and glue. They should be washed after use.

Paints
These must be non-toxic. Different colours can be mixed together to form new ones.

Paper glue
This comes in various formats but is easiest to use when in a tube.

Pencil sharpener
Use this to keep your pencils nice and sharp.

Pins
These are used to hold fabric together when sewing. They are very sharp.

Pom-poms
These can be bought from specialist shops or you can make your own. They can be glued or sewn onto projects.

PVA (white) glue
This must be non-toxic. When undiluted it is very useful for sticking heavy materials together. It can be diluted with water and used for papier-mâché.

Rolling pin
This is used for rolling out salt dough or cookie dough.

Ruler
This is used for measuring and drawing straight lines.

Safety pin
This can be used instead of a badge pin.

Salt
Use large amounts for the basic salt dough mixture.

Scissors
These should not be too sharp and must be handled safely at all times.

flour

salt

felt

crêpe and tissue paper

paints

PVA (white) glue

paintbrushes

cress seeds

rolling pin

scissors

needle and thread

face paints

wax crayons

safety pin

badge pins

glitter

pencil sharpener

coloured sticky-tape

paper glue

pins

ruler

felt-tip pens

pom-poms

coloured pencils

Recyclable Materials

These materials can be found in or around the house. Remember – always ask permission before using materials like these in a project.

Bark
Use tree bark as decoration or take rubbings from it.

Cork
This can be used to make your own stamp block.

Cotton wool (ball)
Moisten with water and grow your own cress garden.

Egg carton
This can be cut up and used in a papier-mâché project.

Fabric
Find scraps around the home and use them in your sewing projects, or use fabric from old clothes.

Foil pie cases (pans)
Fold or cut these up and use as decoration.

Gravel
Fill a container with this and use as a musical shaker.

Ivy
The leaves can be pressed and used to decorate collages and greeting cards.

Juice carton
Use this to make your own periscope.

Matchbox
Remove the matches before using the box and give them to an adult.

Moss
This is found in a garden. When brought inside it will dry out and fade in colour.

Newspaper
Tear newspaper into pieces or use it to cover a work surface.

Paper plates
Use these as paint palettes.

Paper towel tube
This can be cut up into whatever size you need.

Pine cones
These can be turned into tasty bird feeders.

Plastic cups
Use these filled with water to wash paintbrushes.

Raffia
Use straw as an alternative if you can't find any raffia.

Scourers
These are used in the kitchen to clean pots and pans. They make good decorations.

Shells
Shells can be painted or left as they are.

Split bamboo canes
Use these to help make a beautiful bouquet of flowers.

Stones
These come in all shapes and sizes and can be painted.

Straws
Use these for blow-painting.

String
Thread beads onto string to make a necklace.

Sweet (candy) cases and wrappers
These can be flattened and cut into shapes and then used to decorate projects.

Terracotta flowerpots
These may be painted and used to store all kinds of things.

Tin foil
This can be cut into shapes and used as decoration.

Tinsel
Tinsel from the Christmas tree can be used as decoration.

Toothpicks
These are very useful for making holes in salt dough projects.

plastic cups

cork

pine cones

stone

foil pie cases (pans)

moss

egg carton

juice carton

tinsel

split bamboo canes

paper towel tube

paper plates

bark

tin foil

terracotta flowerpots

fabric

shells

gravel

matchbox

cotton wool (ball)

string

toothpicks

sweet (candy) wrappers

ivy

straws

sweet (candy) cases

newspaper

scourer

raffia

TECHNIQUES

Flattening and cutting up a box

Cardboard can be used for papier-mâché frames among other things. Old boxes are the best source, and you can flatten them out easily.

 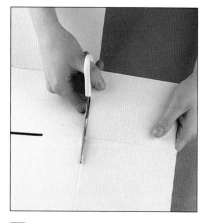

1 Remove any tape that is holding the box together and press it flat.

2 Cut the box into pieces, ready for use in your various projects.

Re-using foil wrappers

Coloured foil is great for decorations, and you don't have to buy it specially. Save old sweet (candy) wrappers and cases made of pretty colours, and cut them into different shapes.

1 Flatten the wrappers and cases and smooth them out. Cut them up for use in your projects.

Removing a label from a bottle

Plastic bottles can be used for all kinds of projects. You will want to wash them thoroughly.

1 Fill a washing-up bowl with some warm water.

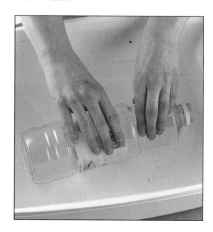

2 Soak the bottle in the water for approximately ten minutes.

3 Peel the label off the bottle.

Papier-mâché

Papier-mâché can be used for all kinds of things. See the projects for ideas, or make your own designs.

YOU WILL NEED
newspaper
PVA (white) glue
bowl
water
wooden stick or paintbrush
vaseline (optional)

1 Tear up sheets of newspaper into small pieces.

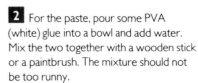

2 For the paste, pour some PVA (white) glue into a bowl and add water. Mix the two together with a wooden stick or a paintbrush. The mixture should not be too runny.

3 If you are covering a balloon apply water or vaseline to the surface and a layer of paper. This will stop the shape sticking to the balloon when you burst it.

5 If you have applied papier-mâché to a balloon, burst the balloon with a pin only when it has thoroughly dried. If necessary, make a small hole and remove the balloon.

6 If you need to add shapes to your mould, fasten them on with two layers of papier-mâché. Leave them to dry completely before painting.

4 For a balloon mould, apply eight layers of papier-mâché and, for a box, about three layers. Paint the surface with the glue mixture and stick on the paper. Leave the papier-mâché to dry completely in a warm place before painting. This may take 24 hours or longer, depending on the number of layers you have used.

Salt dough

Salt dough can be used like clay and baked in the oven until hard. Use this recipe for the salt dough projects in the book.

YOU WILL NEED
300 g/11 oz/3 cups plain flour
300 g/11 oz/2 cups, plus 30 ml/2 tbsp salt
wooden spoon
large bowl
30 ml/2 tbsp vegetable oil
200 ml/8 fl oz/1 cup water

1 Put the flour and 300 g/11 oz/2 cups salt into a large bowl.

2 Add the oil to the flour and salt mixture and add the remaining salt. Mix all the ingredients together with a large wooden spoon.

3 Pour in the water and mix thoroughly, making sure there are no lumps.

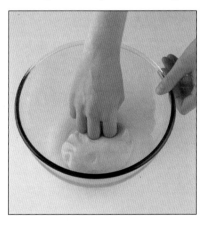

4 Knead the dough until it is firm.

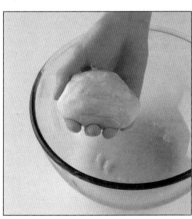

5 When it is ready you can use it straight away or store it in an airtight container in the refrigerator.

16

Tracing templates

Some of the projects in this book use templates that you can trace. To transfer the template to another piece of paper, follow these simple instructions.

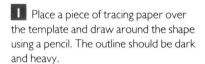

YOU WILL NEED
tracing paper
pencil
card (cardboard) or paper

1 Place a piece of tracing paper over the template and draw around the shape using a pencil. The outline should be dark and heavy.

2 Take the tracing paper off the template and turn it over. Rub over the traced image with a pencil on the reverse side of paper.

3 Place the tracing on a piece of card (cardboard) or paper with the rubbed pencil side facing down. Draw over the lines you have made with a pencil to transfer the picture.

Scaling-up

Sometimes you will want to make a project bigger than the template given. It's easy to make it larger. This is known as scaling-up.

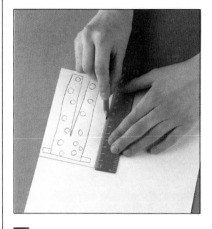

1 Draw a box around your original shape. Draw two diagonal lines through the box and to the top edge of the page.

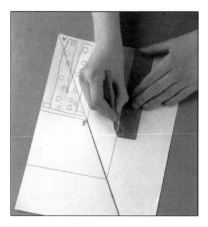

2 Draw a box as large as you want your scaled-up image to be.

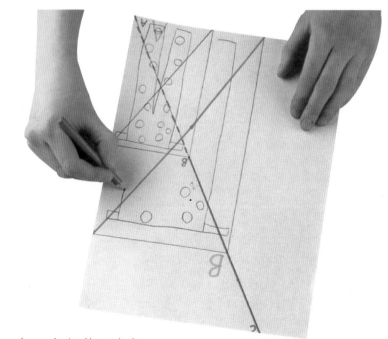

3 Draw the newly-sized image in the box, looking very carefully at the original.

TEMPLATES

*T*hese templates are used in some of the projects in the book.
You can either trace them directly from the page or
make them as large or small as you like.

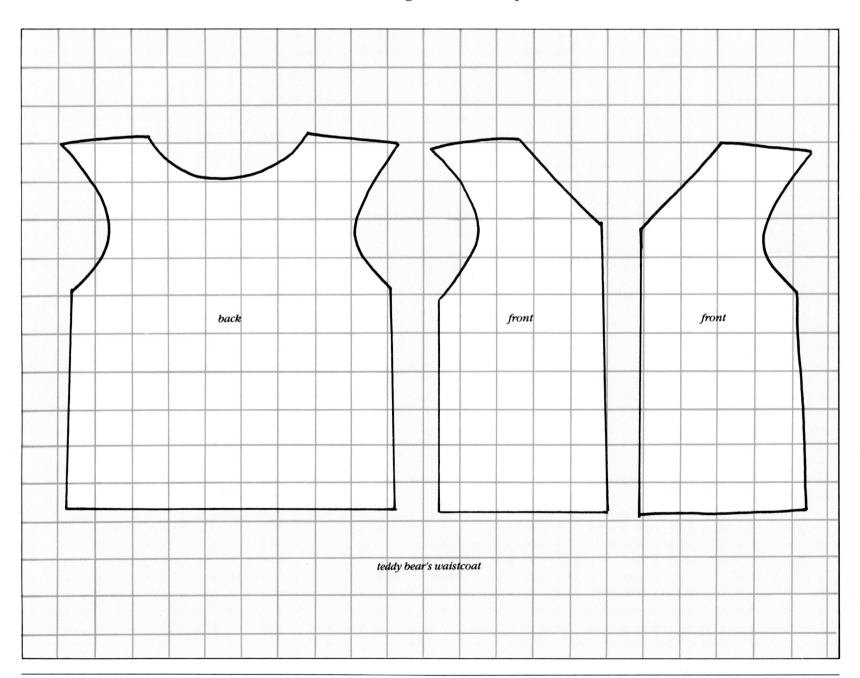

back

front

front

teddy bear's waistcoat

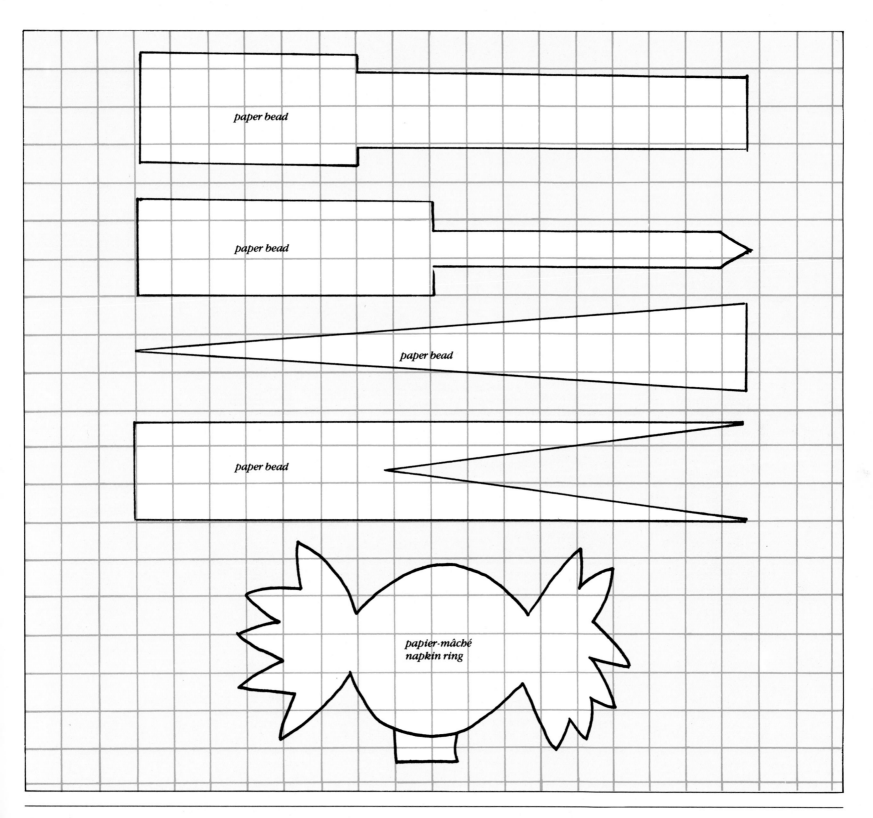

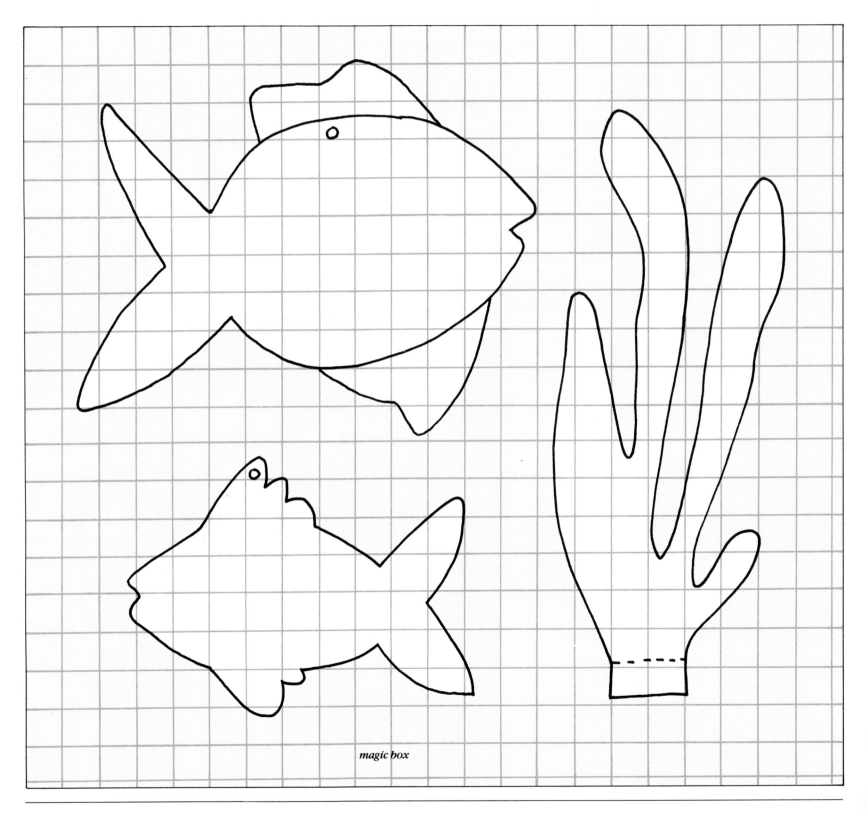

magic box

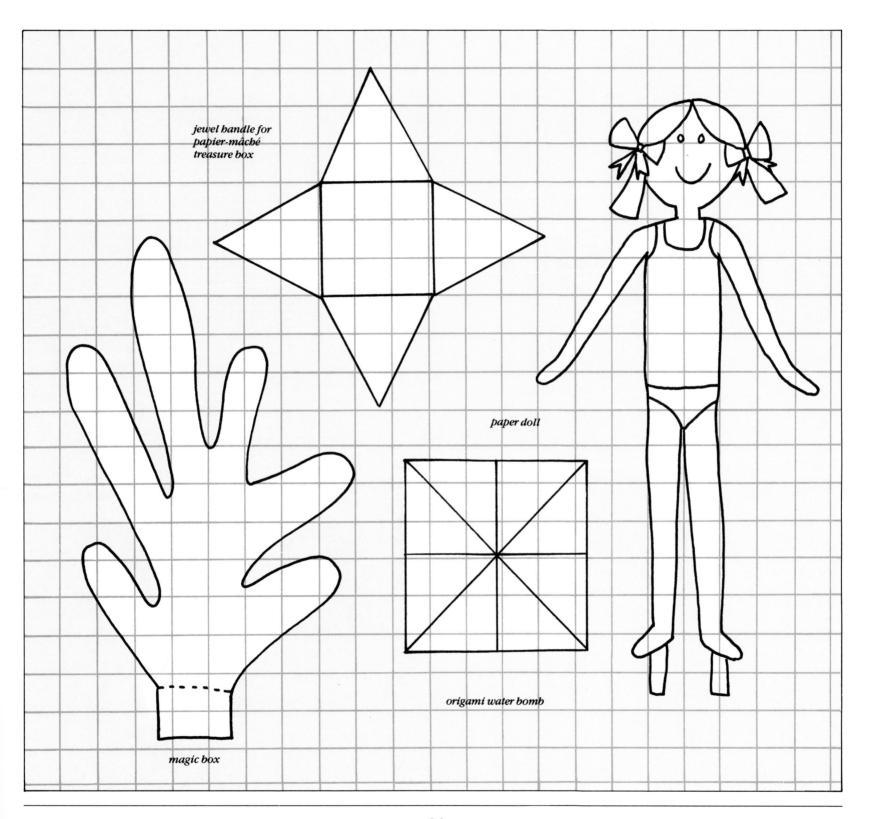

jewel handle for
papier-mâché
treasure box

paper doll

magic box

origami water bomb

PAINTING AND PRINTING

Potato Printing

Create your own wrapping paper with this simple and fun technique.

YOU WILL NEED
potato
knife
felt-tip pen
coloured ink
paper towel
paper plate or saucer for the ink
white or coloured paper

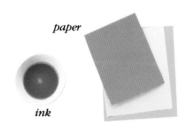
paper

ink

paper towel

knife

potato

paper plate

felt-tip pen

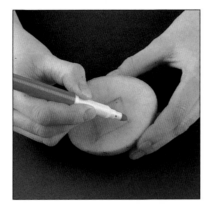

1 Cut a potato in half with a sharp knife and draw out a shape with a felt-tip pen.

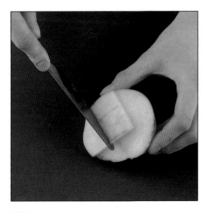

2 With the help of an adult, cut out the area around the shape.

3 Pour a few drops of ink onto a piece of paper towel placed on a paper plate or saucer and dab the potato into it.

4 Place the potato onto some white or coloured paper and press down hard. Repeat this process until the paper is covered with the design.

String Printing

Print this string design on coloured paper and cover
your school textbooks.

YOU WILL NEED
cardboard
scissors
PVA (white) glue
felt-tip pen
string
saucer or paper plate
coloured paints
paintbrush
coloured paper

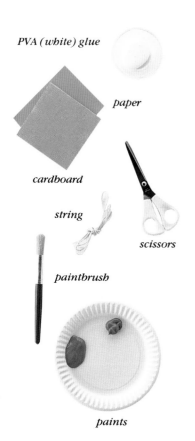

PVA (white) glue

paper

cardboard

string

scissors

paintbrush

paints

1 Cut out a few pieces of cardboard
with a pair of scissors and stick the pieces
together with PVA (white) glue to make
a thick block.

2 Draw a design onto the cardboard
with the felt-tip pen.

3 Cover the cardboard with glue and
stick the string around the outline of the
design. Allow to dry.

4 Dab paint onto the block with a
paintbrush. Press down onto the paper.
Repeat this process until the paper is
covered with the design.

Painting Eggs

The perfect Easter gift for your friends and family.
Put them in baskets or hide them for an egg hunt.

YOU WILL NEED
eggs
pin
small bowl
coloured paints
paintbrush

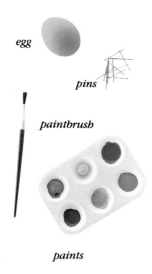

egg

pins

paintbrush

paints

CRAFT HINT

Make a whole batch of eggs in
different colours. You could paint on
names or paint faces to look like your
friends and family.

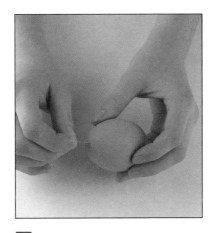

1 Pierce a hole in both ends of each
egg with a pin.

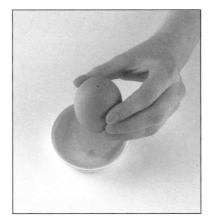

2 Carefully blow the contents of the
egg into a small bowl.

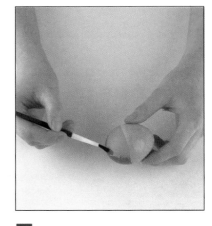

3 Paint one half of the egg and leave it
to dry. Paint the other half in a different
colour if you wish.

4 When the paint is dry, add a
spotty bow.

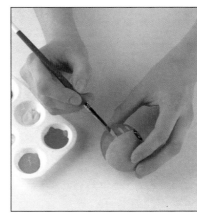

5 When the bow is dry, paint a band
of different colours around the egg.

6 Finish decorating the egg with
coloured spots.

Sponging

This is a fun and easy way to decorate paper.
You could make your own matching cards and
wrapping paper.

YOU WILL NEED
card (cardboard)
felt-tip pen
craft knife or scissors
coloured paints
paper plate or saucer
sponge
coloured paper

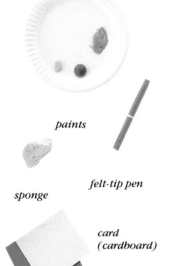

paints

sponge

felt-tip pen

*card
(cardboard)*

paper

IMPORTANT
SAFETY NOTE

You will need an adult to help you cut
out the stencil.

1 Draw the design onto the card
(cardboard) with the felt-tip pen.

2 Ask an adult to help you cut out the
shapes with a craft knife or scissors.

3 Put the paints onto a paper plate or
saucer, and place the cut-out card onto a
piece of coloured paper. Dip the sponge
into the first paint colour and dab it onto
the paper.

4 Repeat this process, washing the
sponge before using each different colour,
until the paper is covered with the design.

Marbling

Cover your books and pencil holders with these beautiful marbled prints.

YOU WILL NEED
newspaper
turpentine
coloured oil paints
plastic cups
wooden stick
washing-up tub or plastic container
cold water
paper

paper

wooden stick

oil paints

IMPORTANT SAFETY NOTE

You will need an adult to help you marble the paper.

1 First of all, cover the work surface with newspaper to avoid too much mess! With an adult's help, pour the turpentine and coloured oil paints into plastic cups and mix well with the stick.

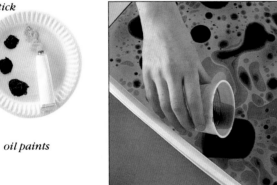

2 Half-fill the washing-up tub or plastic container with cold water. Pour the different-coloured paint mixtures into it.

3 Using a stick, stir the paints to make lots of patterns.

4 Carefully place a piece of paper on top of the mixture inside the washing-up tub for 15 seconds and gently remove. Place your prints on top of some newspaper and allow them to dry.

Painted Terracotta Flowerpots

Store your bits and pieces in these colourful pots, or use them to plant bulbs in the spring.

YOU WILL NEED
terracotta flowerpot
coloured paints (acrylic or emulsion)
paintbrushes
varnish (optional)
PVA (white) glue (optional)

paints

flowerpot

varnish

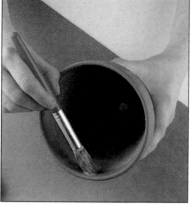
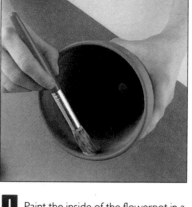

paintbrushes

1 Paint the inside of the flowerpot in a single colour. Allow to dry.

2 Paint the outside rim of the pot in another colour. Allow to dry.

3 Paint the rest of the outside in a third colour.

4 Paint spots on the inside of the pot.

5 Paint stripes on the rim and spots around the rest of the pot and leave it to dry thoroughly.

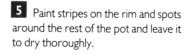

6 Complete the design with more spots. Varnish the pot completely and leave it to dry before using. If you don't want to use varnish, you can use PVA (white) glue thinned with water. Use a paintbrush to cover the pot. It will dry clear, like varnish.

IMPORTANT SAFETY NOTE

Always use varnish in an area where there is plenty of air. Do not breathe in the varnish fumes, and clean your brushes thoroughly afterwards.

Scraper Boards

Create your own exciting work of art with this fun technique. When you scrape away the background, different colours will appear.

YOU WILL NEED
coloured wax crayons
card (cardboard)
washing-up liquid (detergent)
black poster paint
paintbrush
paper clip

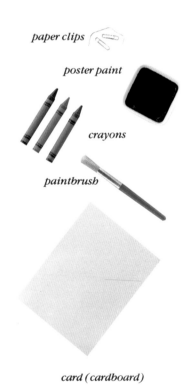

paper clips

poster paint

crayons

paintbrush

card (cardboard)

1 Rub different-coloured wax crayons onto a piece of card (cardboard) until it is completely covered.

2 Mix a few drops of washing-up liquid (detergent) with the black poster paint and paint over the card. Allow to dry.

3 With an opened-up paper clip, scrape your design onto the card. The colours underneath will show through.

Blow Painting

You will be amazed at the beautiful colours and wonderful shapes you can create by using this very simple technique.

YOU WILL NEED
coloured paints
water
plastic cups
paper
straws

plastic cup

paper

straws

paints

1 Mix each different colour of paint together with water in separate plastic cups.

2 Pour drops of the different-coloured paint mixtures onto a piece of paper.

3 Using a straw, blow the paint around the paper to make a pattern.

4 Add more drops of the paint mixture onto the paper and continue blowing until you are happy with the pattern you have made.

Making an Exhibition

Show off your works of art to your friends and family.
You can make tickets to allow entry, and make signs
for each of the paintings.

YOU WILL NEED
card (cardboard)
pencil
scissors
shiny paper in blue, silver and gold
PVA (white) glue
paintbrushes
glitter
ruler

card (cardboard)

glitter

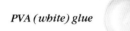

shiny
paper

PVA (white) glue

paintbrush

pencil

scissors

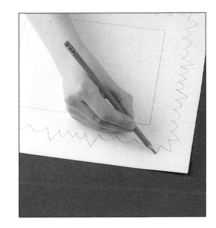

1 Draw the frame onto a piece of card
(cardboard) with a pencil.

2 Carefully cut out the frame with a
pair of scissors.

3 Stick the shiny paper onto the card
frame with PVA (white) glue and cut out.

4 Dab spots of glue around the frame
and sprinkle on the glitter.

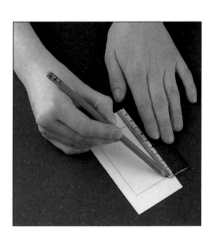

5 For the exhibition tickets, cut out
pieces of card measuring 4 cm × 8 cm
(1½ in × 3¼ in).

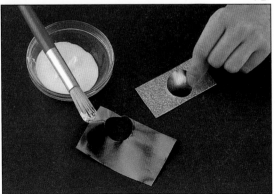

6 Glue silver paper onto the card and cut out gold paper spots. Stick the gold spots onto the silver-covered card. Hang up your paintings and open the exhibition.

Decorated Stone Paperweight

Keep your homework under control with this colourful paperweight.

YOU WILL NEED
large smooth stone
water
pencil
coloured paints
pàintbrush
colourful felt
scissors
PVA (white) glue

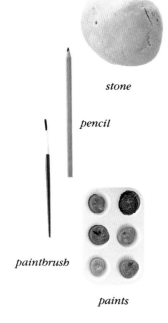

stone

pencil

paintbrush

paints

1 Wash the stone with water and dry it completely before starting to decorate with paints.

2 Lightly draw your picture on the stone using a pencil.

3 Paint the background of the picture onto the stone.

4 Paint on the main picture using lots of different-coloured paints.

5 Finish off the painting with small details and leave to dry.

6 Cut out a piece of colourful felt and stick it onto the bottom of the stone with PVA (white) glue.

RECYCLED PROJECTS

Christmas Stocking

Hang this stocking at the end of your bed for Santa to fill with plenty of Christmas presents.

YOU WILL NEED
paper
pencil
scissors
colourful or patterned fabric
red felt
needle
thread
pins
velvet ribbon
rik-rak braid
PVA (white) glue
paintbrush
buttons

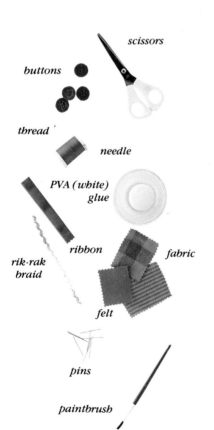

scissors

buttons

thread

needle

PVA (white) glue

rik-rak braid

ribbon

fabric

felt

pins

paintbrush

1 Draw a stocking shape on a piece of paper, and use it as a pattern. You will need to make the pattern 1 cm (½ in) bigger all around to allow for the seam. Cut out 2 pieces of fabric for the main part of the stocking. Cut out a spiky border from red felt for the top.

2 Fold over the top edge of each stocking piece and sew with a needle and thread.

3 Pin the two stocking pieces together making sure the right sides are facing each other. Sew around the bottom and sides leaving a 1 cm (½ in) seam allowance. Turn the stocking right-side out.

4 Pin the red spiky felt around the top edge of the stocking together with a piece of velvet ribbon for the loop, and sew.

5 Stick some more velvet ribbon and some rik-rak braid onto the red felt with PVA (white) glue.

6 Sew some buttons onto the red felt.

IMPORTANT SAFETY NOTE

You may need an adult's help for the sewing. If you don't want to sew, you could make the entire stocking from felt, and glue the sides together with a thin layer of PVA (white) glue.

Advent parcel

Treat yourself with this parcel filled with plenty of surprises for Christmas. Open one section a day until Christmas by carefully punching open the top.

YOU WILL NEED
4 half-dozen egg cartons
card (cardboard)
PVA (white) glue
paintbrush
coloured tissue paper
sweets (candies)
coloured crêpe paper
glitter
coloured and shiny paper
scissors
paints
ribbon
embroidery thread

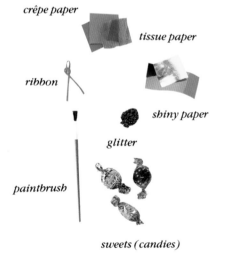

crêpe paper

tissue paper

ribbon

shiny paper

glitter

paintbrush

sweets (candies)

egg carton

1 Stick four egg cartons onto a piece of card (cardboard) with PVA (white) glue. Fill each container with coloured tissue paper and a sweet (candy).

2 Wrap up the parcel with coloured crêpe paper. Dab spots of glue onto the parcel and sprinkle on the glitter.

3 Cut out small circles of coloured and shiny paper, and stick on the top of each egg compartment. Paint numbers on each circle. Wrap a piece of ribbon around the parcel and tie a bow.

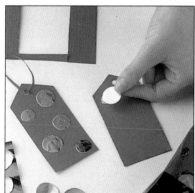

4 Make a gift tag from coloured paper and decorate it with some spots of shiny paper. Tie the tag to the bow with the embroidery thread.

Juggling Squares

Keep practising your juggling skills and impress everyone around you.

YOU WILL NEED
squares of colourful fabric
pencil
ruler
scissors
pins
needle
thread
crumpled paper or newspaper

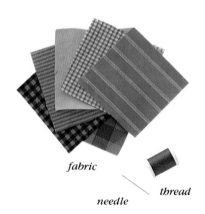

fabric

needle　　*thread*

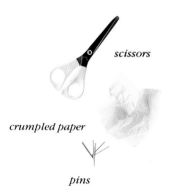

scissors

crumpled paper

pins

IMPORTANT SAFETY NOTE

You may need an adult's help for the sewing.

1 For each juggling square you will need six squares of fabric, 12 cm × 12 cm (4¾ in × 4¾ in). Cut these out with a pair of scissors. With the right sides facing each other sew the first two squares together with a needle and thread, allowing a 1 cm (½ in) seam allowance.

2 Sew all the squares together to form a letter 'T' shape.

3 Join the sides together to form a cube, leaving one side open for the stuffing. Turn the cube right side out.

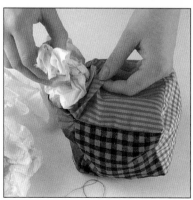

4 Fill the cube with the crumpled paper or newspaper, and, when it is full, sew up the last side.

Salt Dough Badges and Bedroom Wall Plaque

Add your own personal style to your bedroom wall and T-shirts.

YOU WILL NEED
salt dough (see page 16)
rolling pin
card (cardboard) for template
pencil
scissors
knife
baking tray (sheet)
oven gloves
fish slice (spatula)
cooling rack
coloured paints
paintbrush
badge pins
PVA (white) glue

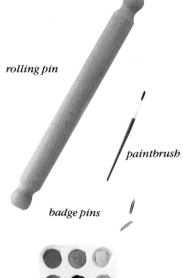

rolling pin

paintbrush

badge pins

paints

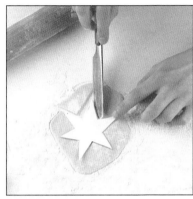

1 Make the salt dough following the instructions on page 16. Roll it out onto a surface sprinkled with flour until it is 5 mm (¼ in) thick. Draw stars and other shapes onto card (cardboard) and cut out. Place the templates onto the dough and cut around them with a knife.

2 Make some small balls and other decorations out of the dough and stick them to the badges.

3 Lay the badges out on a greased baking tray (sheet). With the help of an adult, heat the oven to 100°C/225°F/ Gas ¼ and put in the baking tray. Cook for approximately 6 hours or until they are hard. Wearing oven gloves, remove the tray from the oven. With a fish slice (spatula), slide the badges onto a cooling rack. Allow to cool before painting.

4 Paint around the background in bright colours.

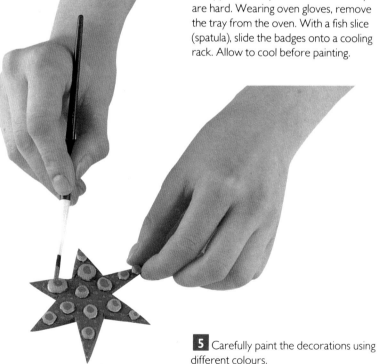

5 Carefully paint the decorations using different colours.

6 Stick the pins onto the back of the badges with PVA (white) glue. Leave it to dry before wearing. Make the wall plaque in the same way as you made the badges, but remember to make a hole in the dough before baking so that it can be attached to your door or wall.

IMPORTANT SAFETY NOTE
You will need an adult to help you to heat the oven and remove the salt dough once it has been baked. Use oven gloves and do not touch the baking tray (sheet) until it has cooled completely.

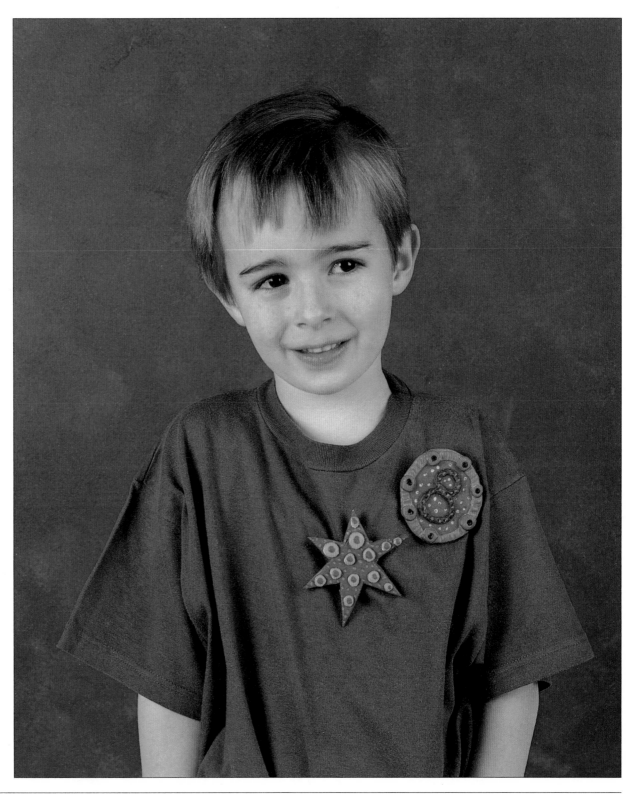

Make your own Garden

Create your own indoor garden paradise within a
cardboard box. If you use moss from the garden you
may need to replace it after a few days if it dries out.

YOU WILL NEED
scissors
ruler
cardboard box
brown paint
paintbrush
small mirror
magazine pictures
bits and pieces from the garden such
 as moss, earth, gravel, ivy and twigs
shells
plasticine

shells

leaves

gravel

moss

ivy

plasticine

mirror

magazine picture

1 With a pair of scissors, cut the cardboard box so that it is just 4 cm (1 ½ in) deep and paint it brown. Allow to dry.

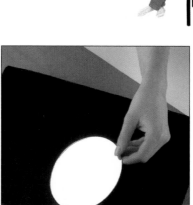

2 For the pond, place the mirror in the bottom of the box.

3 For the garden, arrange the magazine pictures, moss and shells inside the box.

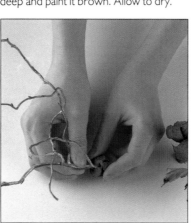

4 For the trees, stick the twigs into a piece of plasticine and place them among the moss and shells.

5 Scatter the gravel and earth to cover any bare patches.

6 Finish off the garden by decorating it with pieces of ivy.

Air Football (Soccer)

A fun game for two or more players. Use the blowers to move the ball into the opposite goal.

YOU WILL NEED
pencil
scissors
card (cardboard) or 2 shoe boxes
masking tape
coloured paints
paintbrush
coloured sticky-back (adhesive) plastic
2 cardboard tubes
ping-pong ball
green sticky-back (adhesive) felt

plastic covering

card (cardboard)

cardboard tube

ping-pong ball

paintbrush

masking tape

paints

scissors

1 Draw the goals onto card (cardboard) and cut out with a pair of scissors, or cut one long side off of each shoe box.

2 Bend back the two short sides about 2.5 cm (1 in) so the goal will stand up. Stick the card together with masking tape if necessary.

3 Paint the goals inside and out. Cut out some spots from the coloured sticky-back (adhesive) plastic and stick them onto the goals.

4 For the blowers, cover two cardboard tubes with coloured sticky-back plastic.

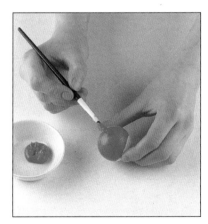

5 Paint the ping-pong ball with bright colours.

6 For the pitch (field), cover a piece of card as big as you like with green sticky-back felt. Mark out the pitch with masking tape and position the goals.

Cress Eggs

These funny eggs have hair that grows. You can give them a haircut and use the 'hair' as a tasty sandwich filling!

YOU WILL NEED
2 eggs
small bowl
cotton wool (ball)
water
cress seeds
coloured paints
paintbrush

cress seeds

egg

paintbrush

cotton wool (ball)

paints

I Carefully crack the eggs in half and empty the contents into a small bowl.

2 Moisten a piece of cotton wool (ball) in cold water and place it inside each egg shell half.

3 Sprinkle the cress seeds sparingly onto the cotton wool. Store the egg shells in a dark place for two days or until the seeds have sprouted, then transfer to a light area such as a windowsill.

4 Paint a jolly face onto each egg shell.

Pine Cone Bird Feeder

Keep your feathered friends fit and healthy with this tasty meal. You can hang it from a tree outside your window and watch the birds flock to eat.

YOU WILL NEED
large pine cone
peanut butter
knife
bird seed
bowl
string

knife

peanut butter

bird seed

pine cone

string

1 Begin to fill the pine cone with peanut butter using a knife.

2 Continue until the cone is completely covered with peanut butter.

3 Pour the bird seed into a bowl and dip the peanut butter cone into it, making sure you completely cover it with seeds.

4 Tie a piece of string around the bottom of the cone. It is now ready to hang outside for the birds.

Post Office

Keep in touch with your friends by running your own post office for letters and packages.

YOU WILL NEED
shoe box
masking tape
felt-tip pen
scissors
coloured paints
paintbrush
corrugated card (cardboard)
coloured paper
PVA (white) glue
string
cork
paper towel
jam jar lid
coloured ink or paint

jam jar lid

paper   *cork*

string

masking tape

paper towel   *PVA (white) glue*

felt-tip pen

scissors

paintbrushes

paints

1 Stick the lid and shoe box together with masking tape. With a felt-tip pen, draw a rectangle on the front of the box and cut it out with a pair of scissors. Paint the box all over with blue paint.

2 Make a jagged-edged decoration and a logo from corrugated card (cardboard) and coloured paper, and stick them onto the front of the box with PVA (white) glue.

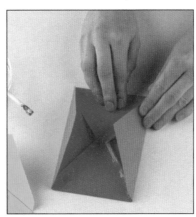

3 Make envelopes from coloured paper. Fold in the three sides and glue them together.

4 For the stamps, cut out small squares of coloured paper and stick different-coloured circles in the middle of the squares. Draw on a small picture using a felt-tip pen.

5 Glue a piece of string around the bottom of the cork to make a pattern.

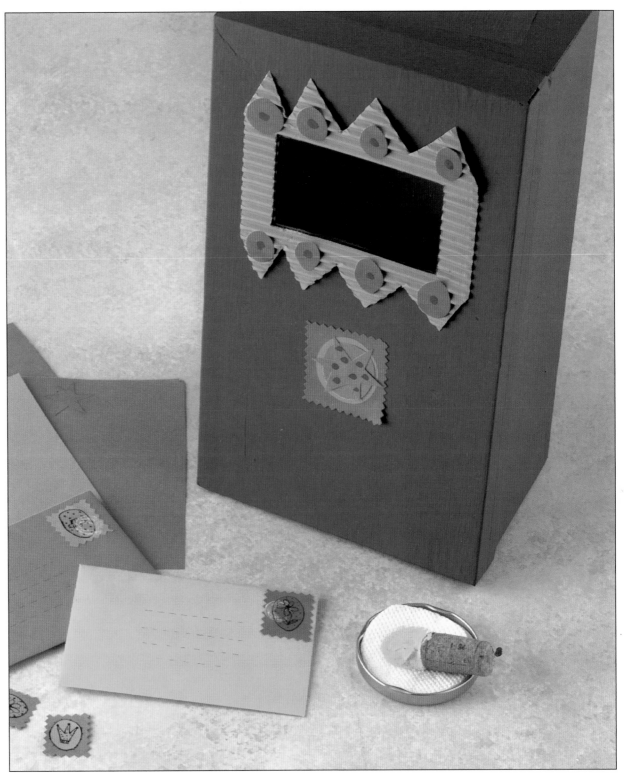

6 Put a piece of paper towel into a jam jar lid and pour on a drop of ink or paint. Dab the cork into the ink-filled lid and then print onto the stamp.

Space Rocket

Travel in time with your very own rocket, made from objects around the house.

YOU WILL NEED
clear plastic bottle
tin foil
scouring pad
scissors
double-sided sticky-tape
shiny paper
PVA (white) glue
paintbrush
tinsel
foil pie dishes (pans)

shiny paper   *pie dish*

sticky-tape
scouring pad
PVA (white) glue
tinsel
scissors
plastic bottle

1 Fill the bottle with scrunched-up pieces of tin foil.

2 Cut the scouring pad in half with a pair of scissors and attach it to the top of the bottle with double-sided sticky-tape. Cut out two spots from the shiny paper and stick onto each side of the pad with PVA (white) glue.

3 Attach a piece of double-sided sticky-tape onto the lid end of the bottle and wrap the tinsel around it.

4 Cut the pie dishes (pans) in half and fold them in half again. Stick to the bottom of the bottle with sticky-tape.

5 Cut out some stars from a piece of shiny paper and stick them onto the bottle with glue or sticky-tape.

6 Cut out two pieces of shiny paper for the wings and glue them onto either side of the bottle.

Musical Instrument

Discover your musical talents with this fun, colourful instrument. You can pluck the string and run the stick over the corrugated paper. You can even hit the top or sides like a drum.

YOU WILL NEED
plain and shiny corrugated paper
cardboard box
PVA (white) glue
felt-tip pen
scissors
coloured paints
paintbrush
tinsel
double-sided sticky-tape
wooden broom pole
coloured sticky-tape
string

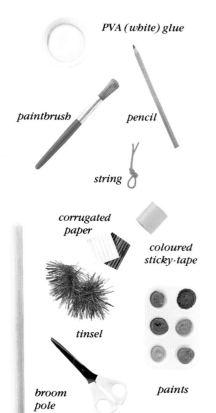

PVA (white) glue

paintbrush   *pencil*

string

corrugated paper

coloured sticky-tape

tinsel

broom pole   *paints*

scissors

1 Stick a piece of corrugated paper around the upright sides of the cardboard box with PVA (white) glue.

2 With a felt-tip pen, draw a circle on one side of the box and carefully cut it out with scissors to make a hole.

3 Glue a piece of shiny corrugated paper on the top of the box. Paint the rest of the box a bright colour.

4 Stick the tinsel around the hole using either glue or double-sided sticky-tape.

5 Paint the wooden broom pole and attach it to the side of the box using coloured sticky-tape.

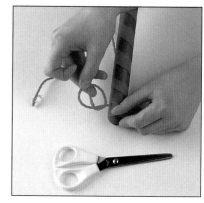

6 Thread the string through the hole at the top of the pole and tie a knot. Make a hole at the top and bottom of the box and thread the string through. Tie a knot to secure. It will need to be very tight to make a noise.

Periscope

The easy way to spy and become a secret agent. Hide behind furniture and walls and look over the top without anyone seeing you.

YOU WILL NEED
tall fruit juice or milk carton
coloured paper
PVA (white) glue
scissors
ruler
pen
2 mirrors
coloured paints
paintbrush

mirror

paintbrush

carton

ruler

scissors

PVA (white) glue

paints

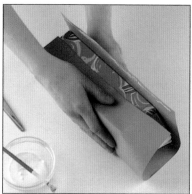

1 Cover the fruit juice or milk carton in brightly-coloured paper.

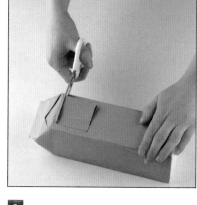

2 Cut out two holes of the same size at the top of the front of the carton and the bottom of the back with a pair of scissors.

3 With a ruler, measure and draw two squares on both sides of the carton, level with the holes on the front and back. Divide the squares with a diagonal line. This is to ensure that the mirrors are at the same angle of 45 degrees.

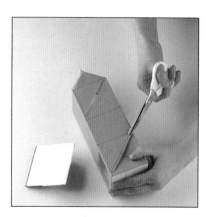

4 Cut a slit along each diagonal line big enough to slide the mirrors through.

5 Slip the mirrors in place with the reflecting sides facing each other.

6 Decorate your finished periscope with painted spots. To use, look through the bottom hole at the back.

54

Matchbox Theatre

This must be the smallest theatre in the world – you can almost carry it in your pocket.

YOU WILL NEED
kitchen matchbox
scissors
coloured paints
paintbrush
coloured paper
felt-tip pen
coloured sticky-tape

paints

paintbrush

kitchen matchbox

scissors

coloured sticky-tape

paper

1 Remove the matches from the box and give them to an adult. Take the matchbox apart and cut one-third off the sleeve with a pair of scissors. Paint both the sleeve and tray and leave them to dry before putting them back together.

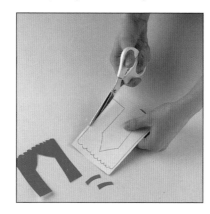

2 Draw the curtains on a piece of coloured paper with a felt-tip pen and cut them out.

3 Attach the curtains to the matchbox using coloured sticky-tape.

4 Paint a face onto the palm side of your middle and index fingers and put them inside the theatre to start acting.

Paper Plate Tennis

A fun game for two or more players to play around the house or outdoors.

YOU WILL NEED
4 paper plates
coloured paints
paintbrush
scissors
coloured sticky-tape
ping-pong ball

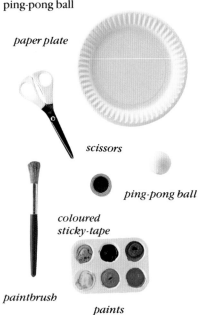

paper plate

scissors

ping-pong ball

coloured sticky-tape

paintbrush

paints

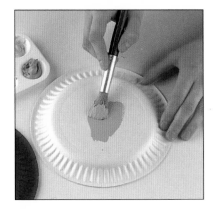

1 For each 'racquet' you will need two paper plates. Paint each plate a plain colour. Allow to dry.

2 Paint patterns onto the plates and leave to dry.

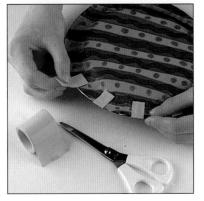

3 Attach the plates with pieces of coloured sticky-tape, leaving a gap big enough for your hand to slide in.

4 Paint the ping-pong ball. Now you are ready to start playing.

Papier-mâché Treasure Box

Keep your favourite treasures hidden away in this box.

YOU WILL NEED
small cardboard box
pencil
scissors
cardboard
PVA (white) glue
paintbrush
tracing and plain paper for template
card (cardboard)
masking tape
water
large bowl
newspaper
wooden stick
coloured paints
foil sweet (candy) wrappers

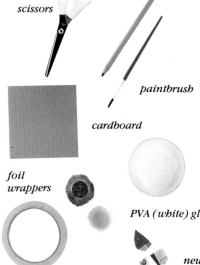

cardboard box

paints

scissors

pencil

paintbrush

cardboard

foil wrappers

PVA (white) glue

newspaper

masking tape

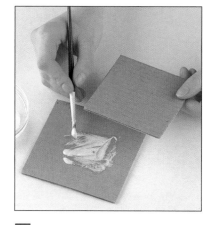

1 For the lid, draw round the box with a pencil on a piece of cardboard and cut it out with a pair of scissors. Cut out a slightly smaller piece and stick this onto the slightly larger piece with PVA (white) glue. Leave to dry.

2 Trace the jewel template from the beginning of the book following the instructions on page 17. Place the template onto the card (cardboard) and cut it out. Bend along the marked lines to join the jewel together and fasten with masking tape.

3 Glue one of the jewel's triangular sides onto the lid.

4 For the papier-mâché, mix some glue with water in a large bowl and stir in several layers of torn-up newspaper with a wooden stick. Apply three layers of papier-mâché to the box and the lid and allow them to dry overnight in a warm place. (This may take a little longer depending on the time of year.)

5 When the box is completely dry, paint the inside and the outside of both the box and the lid. Allow to dry.

6 Flatten the sweet (candy) wrappers and cut out circles from them. Glue the circles onto the box as decoration.

Papier-mâché Piggy Bank

You won't find a friendlier pig to look after your pocket money!

YOU WILL NEED
PVA (white) glue
water
vaseline (optional)
large bowl
newspaper
wooden stick
balloon
pin
egg carton
scissors
masking tape
coloured paints
paintbrush

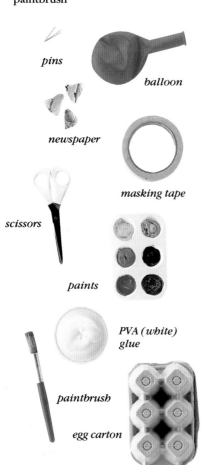

pins

balloon

newspaper

masking tape

scissors

paints

PVA (white) glue

paintbrush

egg carton

1 For the papier-mâché, mix some PVA (white) glue with water in a large bowl and stir in several layers of torn-up newspaper with a wooden stick. Blow up the balloon and tie a knot in it. Cover the balloon with water or vaseline and apply a layer of newspaper, then apply five layers of papier-mâché. Leave the balloon to dry overnight in a warm place. (This may take a little longer depending on the time of year.)

2 Once the papier-mâché is completely dry, burst the balloon with a pin and remove it. You may need to make a small hole to take out the balloon. For the feet and snout, cut up an egg carton with a pair of scissors, dividing up the egg tray and attaching the parts onto the balloon with masking tape.

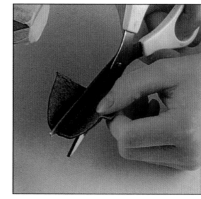

3 Cut out triangles from the egg carton for the ears and attach them to the balloon with masking tape. Use papier-mâché to cover over the feet, snout and ears.

4 For the tail, roll up a piece of newspaper tightly and apply glue to secure it. Wrap the strip around your finger and let go. It should now have a coil shape. Attach it to the balloon with strips of papier-mâché.

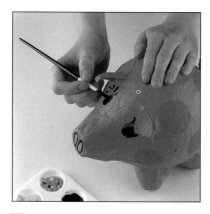

5 When all the papier-mâché is completely dry, apply two coats of paint to the pig.

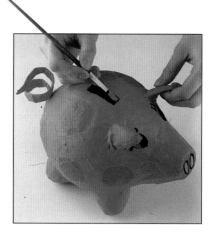

6 Cut out the money slot and finish painting the details onto the pig.

Paper Beads

These fun and colourful beads are made from the pages of a magazine, but no one will guess when you wear them.

YOU WILL NEED
tracing and plain paper for templates
felt-tip pen
scissors
colourful pictures from magazines
PVA (white) glue
wooden stick or knitting needle
embroidery thread

PVA (white) glue

magazine picture

wooden stick

thread

paintbrush

scissors

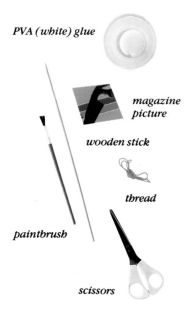

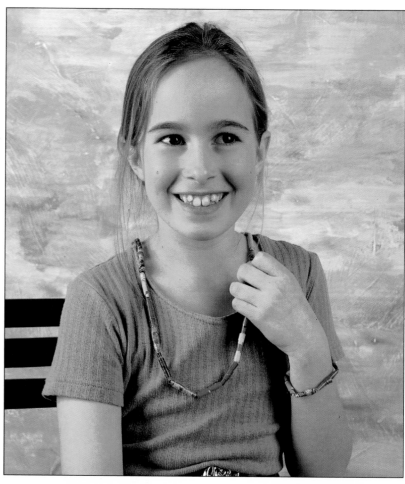

1 Trace the templates from the beginning of the book following the instructions on page 17. Place the templates onto the colourful magazine pictures and draw around them.

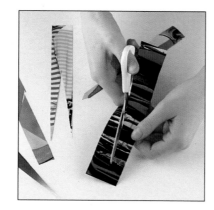

2 Cut out the shapes with scissors.

3 Paint a line of PVA (white) glue in the middle of the shapes and wrap them tightly around a wooden stick or a knitting needle. Carefully remove the stick or knitting needle.

4 When the glue has dried, thread the beads onto a piece of embroidery thread to make either a necklace or a bracelet and tie a knot.

Papier-mâché Napkin Ring

Add some colour to the dinner table with fun napkin rings. You can make your own designs for different occasions.

YOU WILL NEED
tracing and plain paper for template
pencil
scissors
card (cardboard)
PVA (white) glue
cardboard toilet roll
masking tape
water
large bowl
newspaper
wooden stick
coloured paints
paintbrush

1 Trace the sweet (candy) template from the beginning of the book following the instructions on page 17. Place the template onto the card (cardboard) and cut it out. Stick the sweets together with PVA (white) glue. Do not stick the tags because they have to be bent outwards.

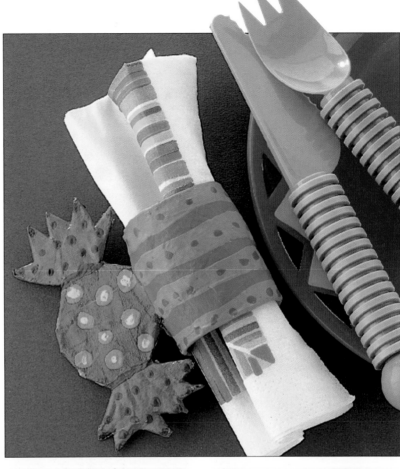

card (cardboard)

newspaper

scissors

paints

paintbrush

pencil

cardboard toilet roll

PVA (white) glue

masking tape

2 Cut a toilet roll in half and attach the sweet to it with masking tape.

3 For the papier-mâché, mix some glue with water in a large bowl and stir in several layers of torn-up newspaper with a wooden stick. Cover the napkin ring with three layers of papier-mâché and leave to dry overnight in a warm place.

4 When completely dry, paint the napkin ring in an assortment of colours and patterns.

Painting Book

Build up a collection of your paintings and drawings in this colourful book.

YOU WILL NEED
coloured paper
ruler
pencil
scissors
needle
thread
scraps of fabric
PVA (white) glue
coloured paints
paintbrush

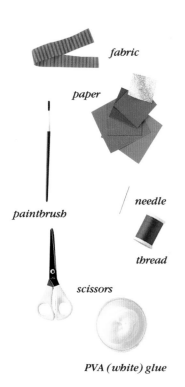

fabric

paper

paintbrush

needle

thread

scissors

PVA (white) glue

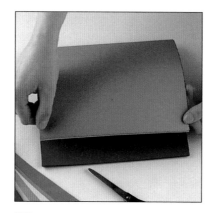

1 For the pages of the book, cut out eight pieces of coloured paper measuring 20 cm × 40 cm (8 in × 16 in). Divide the paper into two piles of four pages and fold them in half.

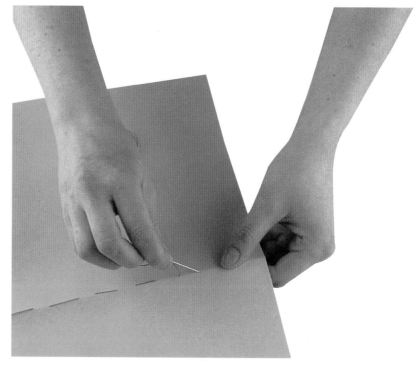

2 Ask an adult to help you sew the first pack of paper together along the centre fold with a needle and thread.

3 Sew the first pack to the second pack along the centre fold.

4 Cut out three strips from the scraps of fabric and stick them onto the two packs of paper with the PVA (white) glue. This will attach them together securely.

5 For the cover of the book, fold a piece of coloured paper measuring 22 cm × 44 cm (8¾ in × 17½ in) in half. Glue this onto the front and back of the pack of paper. Leave to dry.

IMPORTANT SAFETY NOTE

You will need an adult's help to sew the pages of the book in steps 2 and 3.

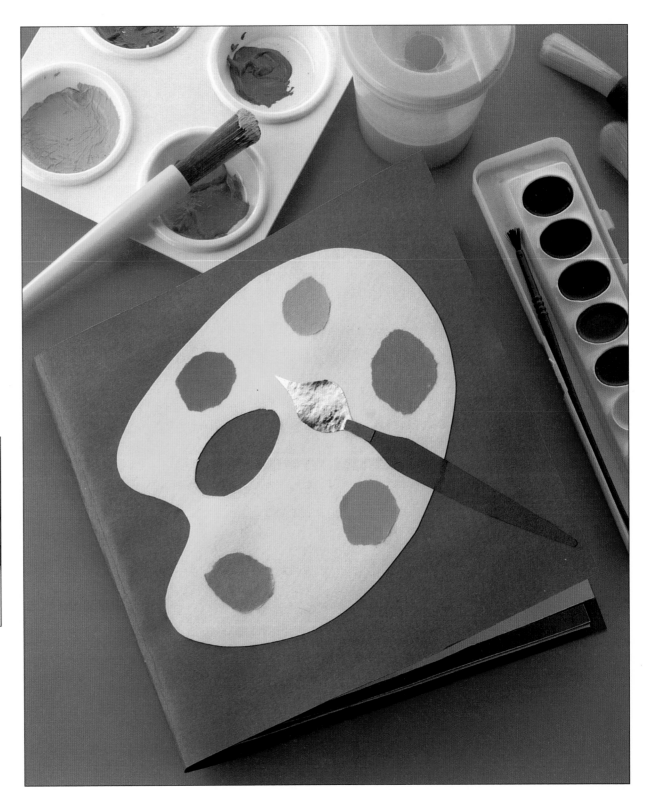

6 Decorate the cover with a paper collage or drawing.

Origami Water Bomb

Seek revenge outdoors with this crafty piece of paper work, but be sure to clear up afterwards!

YOU WILL NEED
pencil
ruler
coloured paper
scissors
water

scissors

paper

1 Measure a piece of paper 20 cm × 20 cm (8 in × 8 in). Cut it out with a pair of scissors. Draw lines across the square following the template at the beginning of the book and fold along them to make creases. Take the two creases either side of the square and pinch them into the centre. Press flat to form a triangle.

2 Fold back the corners of the triangle on both sides to form a square shape.

3 Turn the side corners of the square into the centre. Turn it over and do the same again. Turn the top points into the slots. Turn it over and do the same again.

4 At one end of the bomb there is a small hole. Blow into it hard to make a cube. Through the hole, fill the bomb with water and you are ready to have some outdoor fun!

Origami Basket

Fill this basket with a tasty snack and start munching!

YOU WILL NEED
coloured paper
scissors
coloured paints
paintbrush

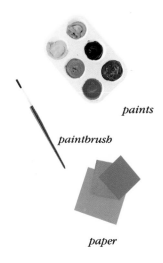

paints

paintbrush

paper

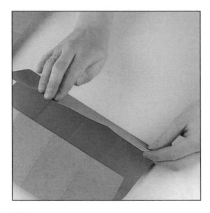

1 Cut out a rectangular piece of paper with a pair of scissors. Divide the paper into 16 squares and fold along the lines to make creases. Fold the short sides to the centre crease of the rectangle.

2 Fold in the four corners as far as the first crease.

3 Fold back the two centre strips over the four triangles.

4 Hold the bowl at the centre points and pull the sides up, then apart. Pinch the corner and bottom creases to straighten them. Paint on your own design.

Paper Flowers

Make your own everlasting blooms of colour. You could use them to decorate gift-wrapped presents or to brighten up a room in a colourful container.

YOU WILL NEED
pencil
coloured crêpe paper
scissors
split bamboo canes
green sticky-tape
plasticine

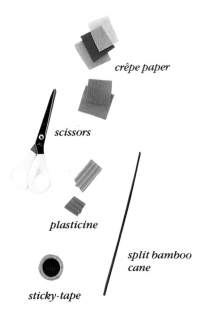

crêpe paper

scissors

plasticine

sticky-tape

split bamboo cane

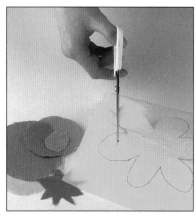

1 With a pencil, draw an assortment of different sized petal shapes onto coloured crêpe paper. Cut them out with a pair of scissors.

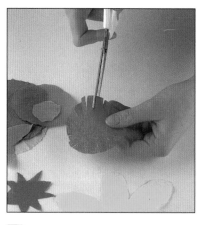

2 Cut around the edge of one of the petal shapes to make a fringe.

3 Starting with the largest petal at the bottom, layer the petals on top of each other, piercing a hole through them with a split bamboo cane.

4 When all the petals are in place, pinch them together and secure with green sticky-tape.

5 Roll a piece of plasticine into a ball and place it in the centre of the cane.

6 Fan out the petals to finish off.

Jigsaw Puzzle

Challenge your family and friends with this home-made jigsaw puzzle.

YOU WILL NEED
colourful picture or large photograph
  of your choice
card (cardboard)
PVA (white) glue
scissors
pencil
paintbrush

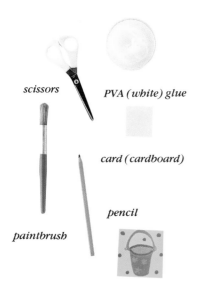

scissors

PVA (white) glue

card (cardboard)

pencil

paintbrush

picture

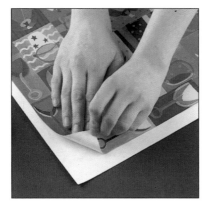

1 Stick your picture onto a piece of card (cardboard) with PVA (white) glue. Rub the palm of your hand over the picture to make sure it is completely smooth. Allow it to dry.

2 Cut around the picture with a pair of scissors to remove the excess card.

CRAFT HINT
You could cut out a picture from a magazine rather than using a photograph.

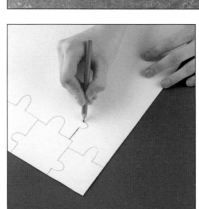

3 Draw the jigsaw pieces onto the reverse of the picture with a pencil.

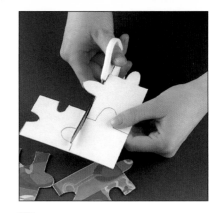

4 Carefully cut out the jigsaw shapes and keep them in a safe place.

Paper Doll

You can make all kinds of outfits for this little doll.
Make some friends and family for her to play with,
or even some pets.

YOU WILL NEED
tracing and plain paper for template
pencil
card (cardboard)
scissors
white paper
coloured paints
paintbrush
shoe box

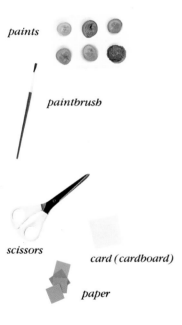

paints

paintbrush

scissors

card (cardboard)

paper

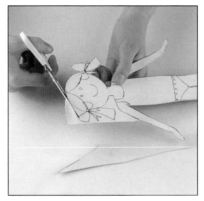

1 For the doll, scale-up the template from the beginning of the book following the instructions on page 17. Trace her onto a piece of card (cardboard). Cut out the doll carefully with a pair of scissors.

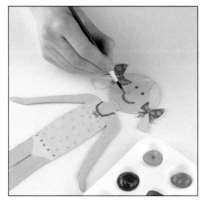

2 Paint the doll's face, hair, and underwear. Leave to dry.

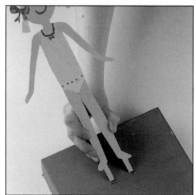

3 Trace around the doll to make the clothes and paint them in bright colours. When you cut out the clothes make sure you leave small tags on them. These will bend behind the doll to stop them from falling off.

4 Paint the lid of a shoe box and make two holes with a pair of scissors to support the doll. Dress up the doll in her various outfits, remembering to bend the tags behind her.

Magic Box

Build your own fantasy world within a box. You could choose any theme you like – a jungle, a circus, or the bottom of the sea, as here.

YOU WILL NEED
coloured paints
paintbrush
cardboard box
scissors
pictures of shells and fish (cut from
    wrapping paper)
PVA (white) glue
netting
blue cellophane
card (cardboard)
pencil
glitter
tracing and plain paper for templates
cotton thread
wooden sticks

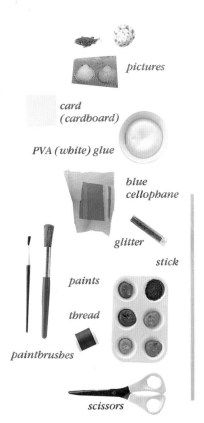

pictures

card (cardboard)

PVA (white) glue

blue cellophane

glitter

stick

paints

thread

paintbrushes

scissors

1 Paint the cardboard box both inside and out. Allow to dry. With a pair of scissors, cut out a rectangle from the top of the box and a circle from the front.

2 Decorate the opening with pictures of fish. Decorate the inside of the box with netting and cut-outs of shells stuck down with PVA (white) glue. Glue a piece of blue cellophane to the back wall.

3 Draw a wave onto a piece of card (cardboard) with a pencil. Cut it out and dab on some spots of glue. Sprinkle glitter over the glue and allow to dry. Cover the wave in blue cellophane.

4 Trace the fish and seaweed templates from the beginning of the book following the instructions on page 17. Place the templates onto a piece of card and cut them out. Paint the shapes in an assortment of colours and leave to dry.

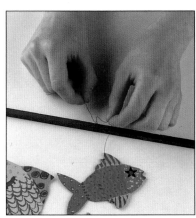

5 Tie a piece of cotton thread to each fish and seaweed shape and tie them to wooden sticks.

CRAFT HINT

If you can't find pictures of shells on wrapping paper look in magazines for pictures. You could also draw your own if you don't find any you like.

6 Place the sticks across the rectangle and dangle the sea-shapes inside the box.

Little Town

Make your own dream town out of small boxes and card (cardboard). Include all your favourite shops, your school and your friends' houses.

YOU WILL NEED
different-sized boxes (matchboxes are
    ideal)
card (cardboard)
scissors
PVA (white) glue
coloured paper
coloured paints
paintbrush
toothpicks
green pom-poms
green glitter
plasticine
green sticky-backed (adhesive) felt

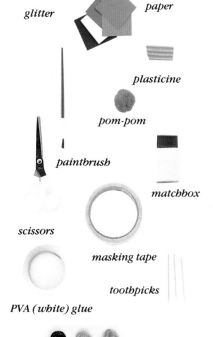

glitter *paper*

plasticine

pom-pom

paintbrush

matchbox

scissors

masking tape

toothpicks

PVA (white) glue

paints

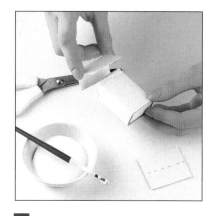

1 Remove the matches from the matchboxes and give them to an adult. For the roof tops of the houses, cut out square pieces of card (cardboard) with a pair of scissors, fold them in half and stick them onto the matchboxes with PVA (white) glue.

2 Cover the houses in different-coloured sheets of paper and paint on doors and windows.

3 For the trees, paint the toothpicks brown. Glue a green pom-pom (see the Clown's Outfit project on page 82 for instructions but substitute fabric with wool) onto a toothpick and cover it in glue. Dab the pom-pom into a ball of green glitter and paint on some red spots. To make the tree stand up, stick it into a piece of plasticine.

4 For the roads, cut out strips of card and paint them.

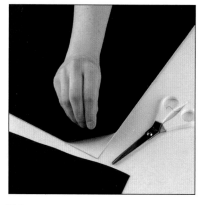

5 Cover a large piece of card with green sticky-backed (adhesive) felt.

6 Arrange the houses, trees and roads around the green felt to create the town. If you don't glue the pieces down, you can change the position of the buildings as many times as you like and store the town away easily.

DRESSING UP

Salt Dough Buttons and Beads

Make your own personalized fashion accessories.

YOU WILL NEED
salt dough (see page 16)
toothpick
baking tray (sheet)
oven gloves
fish slice (spatula)
cooling rack
coloured paints
paintbrush
embroidery thread
rolling pin
tracing paper and card (cardboard)
   for templates
pencil
scissors
knife

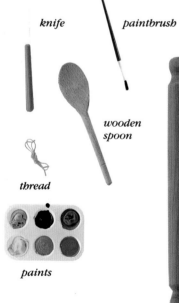

knife　*paintbrush*

wooden spoon

rolling pin

thread

paints

1 Make the salt dough following the instructions on page 16. For the beads, mould a small piece of salt dough on the palm of your hand to form either a round, oblong or flat shape.

2 Pierce a hole through the beads with a toothpick. Lay the beads out on a greased baking tray (sheet). With the help of an adult, heat the oven to 100°C/225°F/Gas 2 and put in the baking tray. Cook for approximately 6 hours or until the beads are hard. Wearing oven gloves, remove the baking tray from the oven. With a fish slice (spatula) slide the beads onto a cooling rack. The beads will be very hot. Allow to cool before painting.

3 Paint the beads in lots of different colours and patterns. Allow each coat of paint to dry before adding the next so the colours don't smudge.

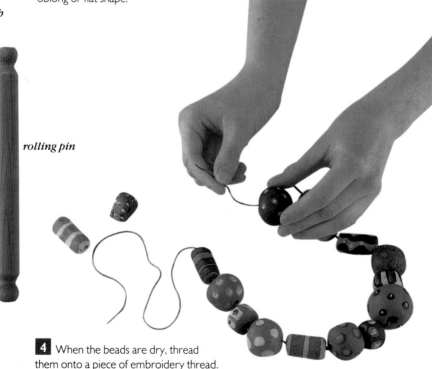

4 When the beads are dry, thread them onto a piece of embroidery thread.

5 For the buttons, sprinkle some flour onto a flat surface and roll out a piece of salt dough until it is 5 mm (¼ in) thick. Trace the templates from the beginning of the book following the instructions on page 17. Place the templates onto the dough and cut around them with a knife. Pierce 4 holes on each button. Bake them in the oven in the same way as the beads in step 2.

You will need an adult to help you to
heat the oven and remove the salt
dough once it has been baked. Use
oven gloves, and do not touch the
baking tray (sheet) until it has
cooled completely.

6 Paint the buttons when cool and
allow to dry. Sew them onto a shirt,
cardigan or even a hat. You will have to
remove them before washing the clothes.
Salt dough should not be washed with
water or in a washing machine.

Vegetable Necklace

Nibble away at this healthy and tasty necklace!

YOU WILL NEED
chopping board
knife
carrots
celery
cabbage
skewer
string
scissors

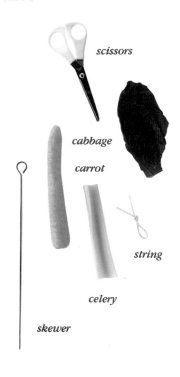

scissors

cabbage

carrot

string

celery

skewer

IMPORTANT SAFETY NOTE

You will need adult help chopping the vegetables and making holes with the skewer.

1 On a chopping board, use a knife to cut the carrots and celery into chunks.

2 Cut the cabbage into triangles.

3 Carefully pierce a hole through the vegetables using a skewer.

4 Thread the vegetables onto a piece of string and cut to the correct length.

Teddy Bear's Outfit

Spoil your teddy with a new set of clothes.

YOU WILL NEED
scissors
colourful felt
needle
cotton thread
ribbon
PVA (white) glue
paintbrush
tracing and plain paper for templates
pencil
buttons
ruler
cotton fringing

thread

needle

PVA (white) glue

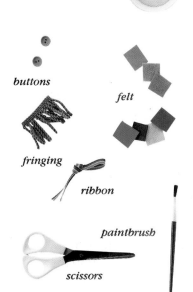
buttons

felt

fringing

ribbon

paintbrush

scissors

1 With a pair of scissors, cut out two semi-circular pieces of colourful felt to fit the width of your teddy's head. Sew the two pieces together with a needle and thread. To decorate the hat, stick on some felt shapes and ribbon with PVA (white) glue.

2 For the waistcoat, scale-up and trace the templates from the beginning of the book following the instructions on page 17. Place the templates onto pieces of felt and cut out. Glue on some felt spots and sew the three pieces together.

3 Sew three buttons onto one side of the waistcoat.

4 For the scarf, cut out a 30 cm × 6 cm (12 in × 2½ in) strip of felt. Glue on strips of coloured felt for the stripes and pieces of cotton fringing for the ends.

Clown Face and Hat

Put a smile on everybody's face with this happy disguise. Complete the costume with the outfit on the next page.

YOU WILL NEED
colourful fabric
scissors
needle
thread
2.5 cm (1 in) bias binding
safety pin
elastic
different-coloured pom-poms or cotton wool balls
PVA (white) glue
paintbrush
coloured face paints

PVA (white) glue

thread

safety pin

needle

fabric

bias binding

elastic

paintbrush

pom-poms

scissors

1 To make the hat, cut out two large circles of colourful fabric big enough to fit over your head, using a pair of scissors. Take a needle and thread and sew the circles together, making sure the right sides are facing and leaving a gap so that you can turn the hat right side out.

2 Sew a piece of bias binding around the circle, 3 cm (1 ¼ in) from the edge. Attach a safety pin to the end of a length of elastic and thread it through the bias binding until it comes out of the other end. Pull the two ends together until the hat is the correct size for your head and tie a knot to secure.

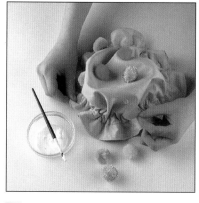

3 Stick different-coloured pom-poms (see the Clown's Outfit project on page 82 for instructions) or painted cotton wool balls onto the hat with PVA (white) glue and allow to dry before wearing.

4 Cover your face with white face paint and paint on a big red nose and rosy cheeks. Colour in your eyebrows.

5 Paint on a large, colourful mouth.

6 Draw a dark outline around your large, jolly mouth.

IMPORTANT SAFETY NOTE

You may need an adult's help for the sewing. When doing the face painting, make sure you use non-toxic face paints specially made to be used as make-up. Some people have a bad reaction to face paints. Try a small amount on a patch of skin before painting your whole face.

Clown's Outfit

This jolly outfit can be worn with the colourful clown face and hat.

YOU WILL NEED
card (cardboard)
pencil
scissors
colourful and patterned fabric
embroidery thread
old T-shirt in a bright colour
cotton fringing
buttons
needle
cotton thread
PVA (white) glue (optional)

scissors

fabric

buttons

needle

thread

fringing

T-shirt

1 For the pom-poms, take two pieces of card (cardboard) and draw two circles onto them. With a pair of scissors, cut out the circles and cut out two more circles from their centres.

2 Put the two circles together. Cut up lots of colourful and patterned fabrics into strips and wrap them around the two circles.

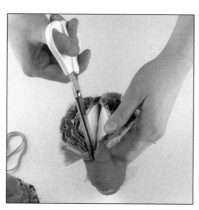

3 When you have almost filled in the hole you can stop wrapping the fabric strips around. Find the pieces of card under all the fabric and put your scissors in between them. Cut around the fabric. Wrap a piece of embroidery thread in between the two pieces of card and tie a secure knot. Tear the card away from the pom-pom and fluff it up, trimming with a pair of scissors if necessary.

4 For the rest of the outfit, find an old T-shirt in a bright colour and sew a piece of cotton fringing around the neckline and the two sleeves.

5 Sew the buttons around the neckline with a needle and thread.

IMPORTANT SAFETY NOTE

You may need an adult's help for the sewing. If you prefer, you can glue all the decorations to the T-shirt, but the costume won't last as long.

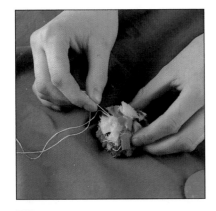

6 Sew on the pom-poms, or stick them onto the T-shirt with some PVA (white) glue.

Spectacular Sea-face

Pretend you've just popped up from the ocean bed with this wonderful design of starfish and seaweed.

YOU WILL NEED
coloured face paints
tinsel wig (optional)

face paints

1 Paint the outlines of the sea-shapes such as fish, seaweed and starfish onto your face.

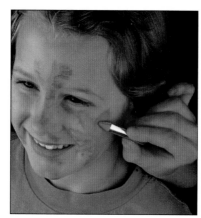

2 Colour in the starfish and seaweed.

3 Fill in the fish with bright colours. Add a mixture of details to them.

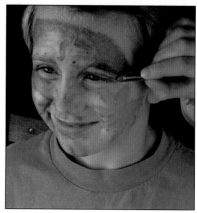

4 Carefully colour in around the shapes so that your whole face is covered with face paints. Put on the tinsel wig, if using.

Tattoo

Wow your friends with this fake tattoo! A butterfly is shown below but you can make any design you like.

YOU WILL NEED
coloured face paints

face paints

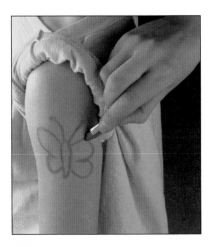

1 Paint the outline of a butterfly or your chosen design onto your arm.

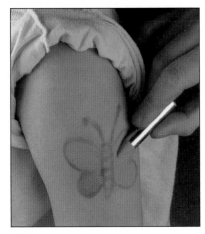

2 Carefully begin to colour it in.

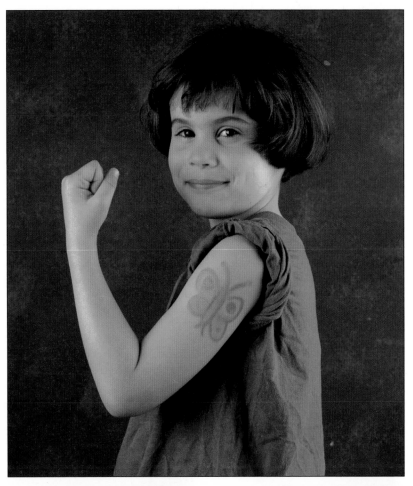

3 Try to make your design as beautiful as possible by drawing tiny patterns and other details.

4 Complete your design. Face paints can smudge very easily, so look after your tattoo and don't let it rub against anything.

IMPORTANT SAFETY NOTE

To remove face paints, check the instructions on the package. They usually come off with soap and water or baby lotion.

Witch Face and Hat

Dress up in this bewitching outfit and cast a spell!

YOU WILL NEED
black paper
scissors
paintbrush
PVA (white) glue
pencil
silver paper
plastic spiders (optional)
raffia
sticky-tape
black and white face paints

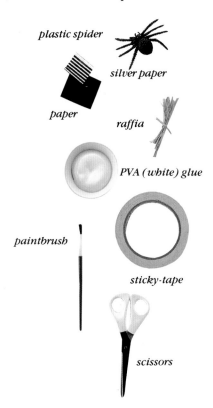

plastic spider

silver paper

paper

raffia

PVA (white) glue

paintbrush

sticky-tape

scissors

1 Cut out a large square of black paper with a pair of scissors. Bend it to make a cone shape big enough to fit your head, before sticking it together with PVA (white) glue.

2 Draw stars onto the silver paper and cut them out. Glue them onto the hat. If you have any plastic creepy-crawlies such as spiders, glue them onto the hat as well.

3 Attach the raffia inside the front of the hat with sticky-tape to make a fringe. Give it a trim if necessary. Make a pair of plaits (braids) and attach them to the inside of the hat with sticky-tape as well.

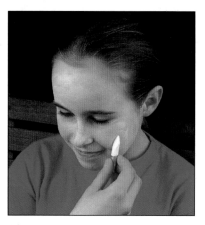

4 Colour your face white with face paints.

IMPORTANT SAFETY NOTE

Some people have a bad reaction to face paints. Test a small amount on a patch of skin before painting your whole face.

5 Draw on some spooky black eyebrows and colour your lips black.

6 Draw a large spider's web on one of your cheeks and cover the rest of your face with black spots.

Regal Crown

Crown yourself King or Queen of the Castle!

YOU WILL NEED
tape measure
card (cardboard)
pencil
ruler
scissors
shiny coloured paper
ribbon
PVA (white) glue
paintbrush
glitter
sticky-tape (optional)

ruler

pencil

glitter

PVA (white) glue

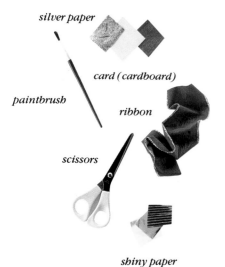

silver paper

paintbrush

card (cardboard)

ribbon

scissors

shiny paper

1 Measure around your head with a tape measure so that you know how long to cut the card (cardboard) band. Remember to allow a few centimetres (inches) for gluing the band together. Cut a strip of card 8 cm (3¼ in) deep with a pair of scissors. Cover the card in shiny paper and stick on a piece of ribbon with PVA (white) glue.

2 Cut out two strips of card measuring 4 cm × 30 cm (1½ in × 12 in) and cover them in silver paper.

3 Make six jewel circles from shiny paper and glitter and glue them onto the ribbon.

4 Attach the silver strips to the inside of the crown band using glue or sticky-tape. If using glue, leave to dry.

5 Trace out five more jewel shapes from card (cardboard) and cut them out with a pair of scissors. Cover each one in gold paper and decorate with circles of shiny paper and glitter.

6 When the jewels are dry, glue them onto the silver bands.

FUN FOOD

Pizza Faces

These funny faces are very easy to make. The base is a crispy crumpet (English muffin) topped with tomato sauce and melted cheese. The toppings are just suggestions – you can use whatever you like to create the shapes for the smiley faces.

YOU WILL NEED
25 g/2 tbsp vegetable oil
1 onion, finely shredded
1 × 7 oz/220 g can chopped tomatoes
25 g/2 tbsp tomato purée (paste)
salt and pepper
9 crumpets (English muffins)
1 × 200 g/7.5 oz packet of processed
   cheese slices
1 green pepper, seeded and chopped
   into small pieces
4–5 sliced cherry tomatoes

crumpet (English muffin)

onion

tomato purée (paste)

cheese slices

chopped tomatoes

IMPORTANT SAFETY NOTE

Make sure an adult helps make the sauce. Stand away from the frying pan so the hot oil doesn't splash out.

1 With the help of an adult, preheat the oven to 200°C/425°F/Gas 7. Heat the oil in a large pan, add the onion and cook for about 2–3 minutes.

2 Add the can of tomatoes, tomato purée (paste) and salt and pepper. Bring to a boil and cook for 5–6 minutes until the mixture becomes thick and pulpy. Leave to cool.

3 Lightly toast the crumpets (English muffins) under the grill (broiler). Lay them on a baking tray (sheet). Put a heaped teaspoonful of the tomato mixture on the top and spread it out evenly. Bake in the preheated oven for 25 minutes.

4 Cut the cheese slices into strips and arrange them with the green pepper and the cherry tomatoes on top of the pizzas to make smiley faces. Return to the oven for about 5 minutes until the cheese melts. Serve the pizzas while still warm.

Roly Poly Porcupines

A meal in itself! Everyone loves frankfurter sausages (hot dogs) and they're especially good if skewered into hot baked potatoes. Always serve with a big bowl of tomato ketchup nearby.

YOU WILL NEED
4 large baking potatoes
6–8 frankfurter sausages (hot dogs)
50 g/2 oz cherry tomatoes
50 g/2 oz mild Cheddar cheese
2 sticks celery
toothpicks

TO SERVE
iceberg lettuce, shredded
small pieces of red pepper and black olive
1 carrot, chopped

potato

celery

cherry tomatoes

frankfurter sausages (hot dogs)

Cheddar cheese

IMPORTANT SAFETY NOTE

You may need an adult to help chop the vegetables. Make sure an adult takes the potatoes from the oven, and leave them to cool for a while before touching.

1 With the help of an adult, preheat the oven to 200°C/400°F/Gas 6. Scrub the potatoes and prick them all over. Bake in the oven for 1–1¼ hours until soft.

2 Meanwhile, prepare the frankfurters (hot dogs). Heat the frankfurter sausages in a large pan of boiling water for 8–10 minutes until they are warmed through. Drain and leave to cool slightly.

3 Cut the cherry tomatoes in half and when cool enough to handle, chop the sausages into 2.5 cm (1 in) pieces. Cut the cheese into cubes and slice the celery. Arrange them onto toothpicks.

4 When the potatoes are cooked, remove them from the oven. Pierce the skin all over with the toothpicks topped with the frankfurters, cheese cubes, cherry tomatoes and celery slices. Serve on shredded lettuce and decorate the porcupine's head with pieces of red pepper and olive, and a carrot snout.

Kooky Cookies

Easy to make and yummy to eat! Let your imagination run wild with the decorating. If it's easier, you can use coloured icing pens.

YOU WILL NEED

115 g/4 oz/1 cup self-raising (rising) flour

5 ml/1 tsp ground ginger

5 ml/1 tsp bicarbonate of soda (baking soda)

50 g/4 tbsp granulated sugar

50 g/2 oz/4 tbsp softened butter

25 g/2 tbsp golden syrup (light corn syrup)

ICING

115 g/4 oz/½ cup softened butter

250 g/8 oz/2 cups sifted icing (confectioners') sugar

5 ml/1 tsp lemon juice

few drops of food colouring (optional)

coloured icing pens

brightly coloured sweets (candies)

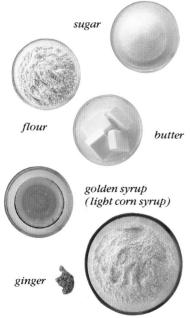

sugar

flour

butter

golden syrup (light corn syrup)

ginger

icing (confectioners') sugar

1 Sift the flour, ginger and bicarbonate of soda (baking soda) into a bowl. Add the sugar, then rub in the butter with your fingertips until the mixture resembles fine breadcrumbs.

2 Add the golden syrup (light corn syrup) and mix to a dough. Preheat the oven to 190°C/375°F/Gas 5.

3 Roll out to 3 mm (⅛ in) thick on a lightly-floured surface. Stamp out the shapes with biscuit (cookie) cutters and transfer to a lightly greased baking tray (sheet). Bake for 5–10 minutes before transferring to a wire rack to cool.

4 To make the icing, beat the butter in a bowl until light and fluffy. Add the icing (confectioners') sugar a little at a time and continue beating. Add lemon juice and food colouring (if using).

5 Spread the icing over the cooled cookies and leave to set.

6 When the icing has set, make patterns on the icing with coloured icing pens and decorate with coloured sweets (candies).

Jolly Orange Boats

These are so easy to make and fun to eat. The only difficult thing is waiting for the jelly (gelatine) to set! These boats make a yummy dessert or party treat. You could serve with ice cream for something extra special.

YOU WILL NEED
2 oranges
1 packet orange-flavoured jelly
   (gelatine)
4 sheets rice paper or coloured paper
toothpicks

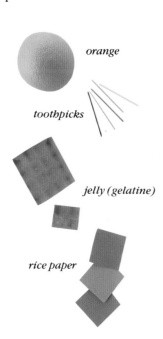

orange

toothpicks

jelly (gelatine)

rice paper

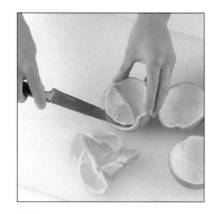

1 Cut the oranges in half lengthways. Scrape out the flesh, taking care not to pierce the skins. Chop up the flesh.

2 Make the jelly (gelatine) according to the packet instructions. Add the orange flesh while the jelly cools.

IMPORTANT SAFETY NOTE

You may need an adult's help cutting the oranges. Be very careful whenever you handle knives.

3 Place the orange shells onto a baking tray (sheet) and pour in the jelly mixture. Leave for 1 hour to set. Once set, cut the skins in half again using a sharp knife to create little boats.

4 Cut the rice paper or coloured paper sheets into eight squares. Pierce each corner with a toothpick and attach the sail to the middle of the orange boat.

Chocolate Witchy Apples

These chocolate witches are great fun. Be careful with the melted chocolate, though, as it has a nasty habit of getting everywhere!

YOU WILL NEED
6 small eating apples
6 wooden lollipop sticks
250 g/8 oz/8 squares milk chocolate
6 ice cream cones
sweets (candies) for decorating

apple

milk chocolate

sweets (candies)

lollipop stick

ice cream cone

IMPORTANT SAFETY NOTE

Melted chocolate is very hot! Make sure an adult helps you melt it.

1 Peel and thoroughly dry the apples. Press a wooden lollipop stick into the core of each one.

2 In the microwave or over a pan of boiling water, gently melt the chocolate.

3 When melted, tilt the pan and dip the apple into it, coating it thoroughly. Place it on a baking tray (sheet) lined with baking paper. Press the sweets (candies) into the chocolate to decorate before the chocolate sets.

4 Holding the stick, use a little melted chocolate to attach the cone for a hat. The cone can also be decorated by sticking sweets on with spare melted chocolate. Repeat with the other five apples.

INDEX